# I LOVE YOU TO THE STARS AND BACK

## Michael F. Mascia, MD, MPH

Illustrated by Karine Makartichan

To order additional copies of this book, contact:
Xlibris
844-714-8691
www.Xlibris.com
Orders@Xlibris.com

ISBN:  Softcover    978-1-6641-3944-2
       EBook        978-1-6641-3943-5

Print information available on the last page

Rev. date: 11/09/2020

I LOVE YOU TO THE STARS AND BACK

Dedicated to Frankie, Bea, Ben, Jonathan
And all children of all ages
Never underestimate the power of Love.
With Love,
From Pop


"Life IS Love. Anything else is just passing time."

I
LOVE
YOU!!

and that is a **HUGE** Lot of Love

No Matter Where you are,
No matter what you do,
All the day and
All the night,
I Love YOU,
with all my might!

Next sunny day,
Ready to play?
When you swim in the pool,
When you play ball,
When you trip and fall,
When you climb a big rock,
When you need a hug,
When you roll on the rug,
When you run in the park,
When the doggie does bark,
When it gets dark
And the stars start to twinkle,
When eating your food
And drinking your drink
I am always thinking...
Of YOU!

When you head
out to school

When the crickets sing,
When cold winds blow,
When leaves turn bright
and start to glow,
And flutter and dance
in the breeze below
And shake and fall
before the snow
And chase each other
around the trees.

And when it
starts to snow
And you catch
some flakes,
they melt, you know.

"When day is done, you've had your fun,
you know it's best to take a rest.
Pitch black outside ... no more sun.
You go in and stars come out,
Shhhhh ... No more time to run and shout.
Not today. Tomorrow is another day.
Brush your teeth, use the potty,
change your clothes and wash your nose ... it's not so snotty.
Quietly, slowly, crawl Into your bed and under the sheets.
Yes, it's time to rest your head.
Cozy ... tidzy ... stay ... still ... don't get dizzy.
Mom & Dad and all might read a book and tell a story.
Lights out. Dream about the morning, glory.
Do you find ... ideas are dancing in your mind?
Before you fall ... Asleep?"

# My Love

Shines on you like the warm sunshine,
Glows in the dark like the moonlight,
Twinkles in your eyes like the stars in the sky,
Sprinkles on you like the warm raindrops,
Swings, twists, tumbles and turns like leaves
falling … gently … quietly to the ground below,
Sways and dances like the trees that blow in the breeze,
Floats gently down like the big spring snowflakes
that fall on you in the last winter storm,
Trickles in to fill the warm sweet air and… tickles your fancy,
like a gentle rain, bursting with the smell of flowers,
the sound and sights of birdsong, bumblebees,
dragonflies, hummingbirds, grasshoppers,
jumping frogs and butterflies that flutter by
and the taste of your first ripe strawberry.
My Love is always with you.

THE END?
NO! NO! NO!
THIS IS JUST THE START!!

"When you journey through this life,
look into your heart.
Love will show you
COMPASSION!
and
COOPERATION!
two very important parts.
And
When you find you've lost your way,
Makes no difference, night or day.
Just play.
And
Remember, you are not alone.
Wait ... wait ... hold your horses! STOP!!
It is not too late.
Watch the sun fade from the sky while the stars roll in.
Soon you'll see, not just me,
The Big Dipper ...
and
The Little Dipper ...
will be
pointing, pointing to Polaris ...
The North Star,
And that will bring you back on track."

```
C
LOVE
M
P
A
S
S
I
COOPERATION
N
```

https://apod.nasa.gov/apod/ap991006.html

# Note to Parents

ON LOVE

Love has empowered compassion, cooperation and progress among humans since the dawn of our species.

For Further Information

SuperCooperators: Altruism, Evolution, and Why We Need Each Other to Succeed
Martin A. Nowak

https://books.google.com/books/about/SuperCooperators.
html?id=icuUApNfFrMC&printsec=frontcover&source=kp_read_button

On Polaris: The North Star

Pointed to by The Big Dipper and The Little Dipper, Polaris, The North Star has been guiding human travelers for centuries.
You can see Polaris in the northern hemisphere of the earth on any clear night.

For Further Information
https://starchild.gsfc.nasa.gov/docs/StarChild/questions/question64.html

Questions for the author?
Email: mfmascia@gmail.com

Printed in the United States
By Bookmasters